1·2·3 Draw

Cars, Trucks, and Other Vehicles

A Step-by-Step Guide

by Freddie Levin

PEEL PRODUCTIONS, INC.

Before you begin, you will need:

- a pencil
- an eraser
- a pencil sharpener
- lots of paper (recycle and reuse!)
- colored pencils
- a folder for saving work
- a comfortable place to draw
- good light
- a ruler or straight edge
- a circle template or a compass for drawing circles

Now, let's begin...!

Library of Congress Cataloging-in-Publication Data
Levin, Freddie.
  1-2-3 draw cars, trucks, and other vehicles: a step by step guide / by Freddie Levin. p.
  cm.
  Summary: Provides instructions for drawing a variety of cars, trucks, construction
  equipment and other vehicles.
  ISBN 0-939217-44-9 (pbk.)
  1. Motor vehicles in art--Juvenile literature. 2. Drawing--Technique--Juvenile literature.
  [1. Motor vehicles in art. 2. Drawing--Technique.] I. Title: One-two-three draw cars,
  trucks, and other vehicles. II. Title: Cars, trucks, and other vehicles. III. Title.

NC825.M64 L48
743'.896292--dc21   2001045839

Distributed to the trade and art
markets in North America by

NORTH LIGHT BOOKS,
an imprint of F&W Publications, Inc.
4700 East Galbraith Road
Cincinnati, OH 45236

(800) 289-0963

Contents

Important Drawing Tips

1 Draw lightly at first (SKETCH!), so you can erase extra lines.

2 Practice, practice, practice so you can get better and better!

3 Have fun drawing cars, trucks, and other vehicles!

Simple Shapes

All of the vehicles in this book are created with simple shapes.

A **square** has four equal sides.

A **rectangle** has four sides; two sides are longer.

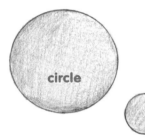

A **circle** is round. (see page 5: About drawing circles)

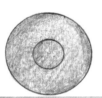

Wheels are circles. First, draw a light line to represent the ground. Then, draw the wheels touching the line.
If both wheels are touching the line, they will be even. Draw the line lightly so you can erase it later.

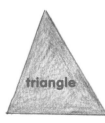  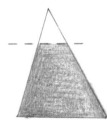 

A **triangle** has three sides and three points. If you chop off one of the points, you have a **trapezoid.**

Drawing Circles and Lines

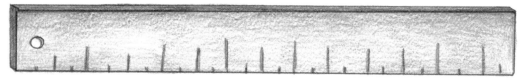

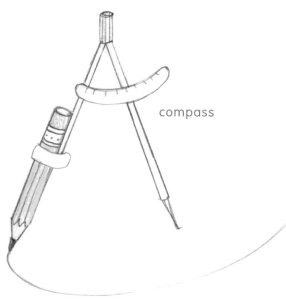

compass

Drawing circles and straight lines is hard and takes a lot of practice. To help you draw straight lines, you can use a ruler or straight edge.

To help you draw circles, you can use a **compass** or **circle template**. Both the compass and the circle template are available at art supply or office supply stores.

A **compass** is a tool with a point and a holder for a pencil. You put the point onto the paper and twirl the pencil around the point to create a circle.

A **circle template** is a plastic stencil with different size circles. You can also use coins, the bottoms of empty cups or containers, or anything you find that is round and the right size.

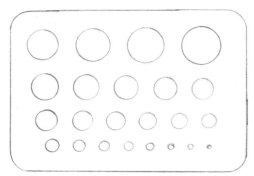

circle template

Sedan

A sedan is a four-door passenger car.
It can seat five people and has a roomy trunk.

1 Sketch a long **rectangle** to start our first car.

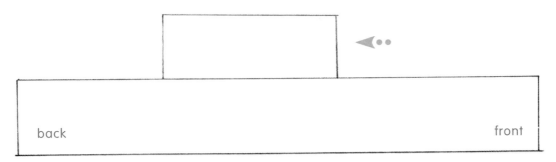

back   front

2 Draw a second **rectangle** on top of the first one. Notice that it is
not in the middle but set toward the back of the car.

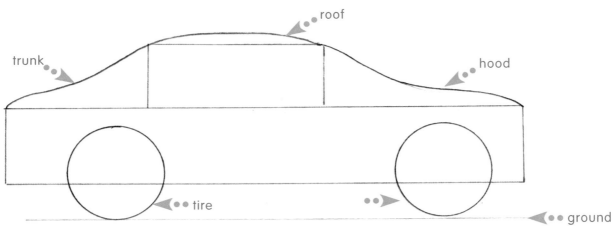

3 Draw a long curving line, using the second rectangle as your
guide, to make the trunk, roof, and hood. Draw a light line for the
ground. Draw two tires touching the line. Notice the positions of
the tires. The back tire is just to the left of the rectangle and the
front tire is closer to the front of the car.

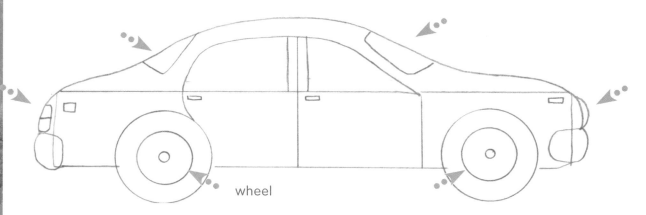

wheel

4 Draw the round back of the car. Add a bumper, a tail light and reflector. Draw the round front of the car. Add a bumper and a headlight. Draw windows, doors, and door handles. Add wheels.

5 LOOK at the final drawing! Erase extra lines. Shade and color. Make your car any color you want!

Convertible

A convertible is a sporty car with a top that can be removed. Some convertible roofs are folded down by hand while some work automatically. Others must be removed completely. A convertible often has no back seat. It's fun to drive when the weather is nice. When it's cold or rainy, it's time to put the top up!

1 Sketch a **rectangle**.

2 Draw lines to round off the front and back of the convertible. Sketch a light line for the ground. Draw two tires touching the line.

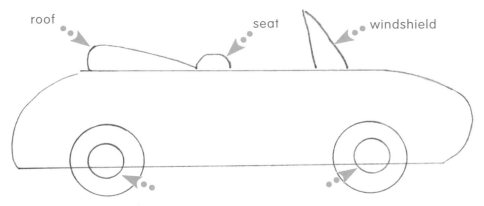

Draw the folded down top of the convertible. Draw the seat just sticking up over the top line of the car. Draw the windshield. Round out the back and front of the car. Draw the wheels.

4 Add the door lines. Draw a curved line for the wheel wells.

5 On the back of the car, add a taillight and a bumper. On the front of the car, add a headlight and a bumper. Draw a door handle. Draw a line of trim along the bottom of the car.

6 LOOK at the final drawing! Erase extra lines. Shade and color your convertible a bright, sporty red.

Cool convertible!

Race Car

Race cars are shaped for speed. The tires are big and the whole car is low to the ground.

trapezoid

1 Sketch a small, thin **rectangle** and a large **trapezoid**. (See how a **trapezoid** is a triangle with one point cut off?)

2 Sketch a line for the ground. Draw large tires.

3 Draw the shape of the back of the car. Add the wheels.

roll cage

4 Draw a "U" shape to form the roll cage (to protect the driver if the car flips). Draw two lines at an angle to make a place for the tailpipes. Add stripes along the bottom of the car. Draw a stripe at the front of the car.

5 Draw a seat for the driver. Add two tailpipes. Draw a stripe in the middle of the car underneath the windshield.

6 LOOK at the final drawing! Erase extra lines. Shade and color your race car.

Ladies and gentlemen, start your engines....

Limousine

A limousine is a long car that can carry many people. When we think of limousines, we think of rock stars and movie stars, but other people hire limousines for special events such as weddings and proms. The driver of the limousine is called a "chauffeur" (show-fer).

1 To start your limousine, sketch a long, thin **rectangle**.

2 Draw two tires.

3 Draw lines to round off the back and front of the limousine. Draw two bumpers.

4 Draw the roof of the limousine. Draw a tail light and reflector on the back of the car. Draw a headlight on the front of the car. Add wheels to the tires.

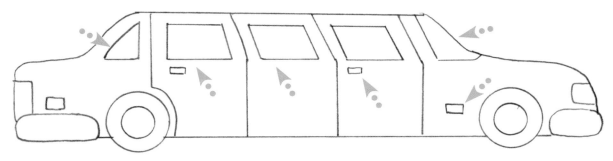

5 Draw the front reflector, windows, doors and door handles.

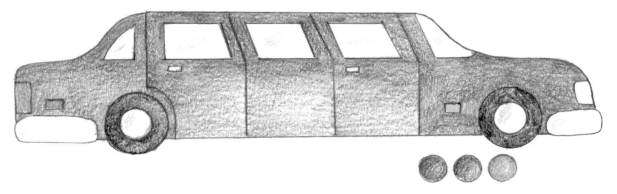

6 LOOK at the final drawing! Erase extra lines. Shade and color your deluxe limo.

Old-fashioned Car

This car was made in the early 1900s. Then cars were a new invention that many people called "horseless carriages." They were slow and not very comfortable. Now cars like this are treasured by collectors and museums, and are an important part of our history.

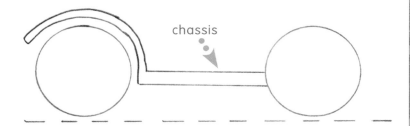

1   To start this old-fashioned car, sketch a ground line. Draw two tires on the line. Add the bottom of the chassis (cha - see) which is the frame of the car.

2   Add the front of the car (hood) where the motor will go. Draw the wheels and hubs.

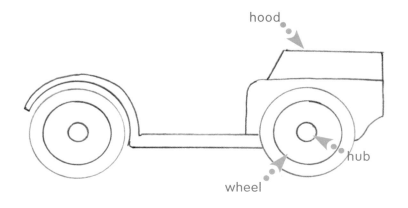

3   On the back of the car, draw the shape for the seat and the supports for the top. On the front of the car, draw a windshield, a knob on the hood, and a head lamp.

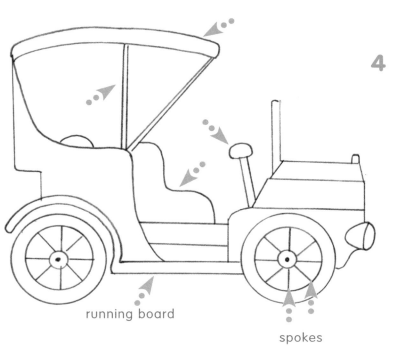

4 Draw the top cover with rods for supports. Draw the seats and the platform called a "running board." Add a "steering stick." Carefully draw spokes in the wheels.

running board

spokes

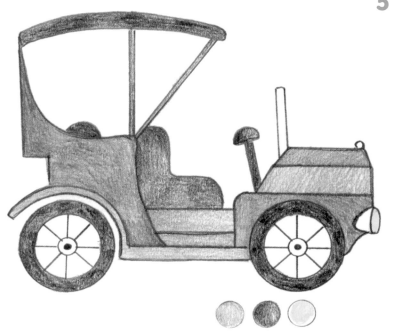

5 LOOK at the final drawing! Erase extra lines. Shade and color your old-fashioned car.

Quaint car!

Taxicab

When you need a ride and don't have a car, you can hire a taxicab. Taxi drivers take people many places. The farther the trip and the longer it takes, the more the taxi driver charges. People take cabs most often in busy downtown areas and to airports when they travel.

1 Sketch a **rectangle**.

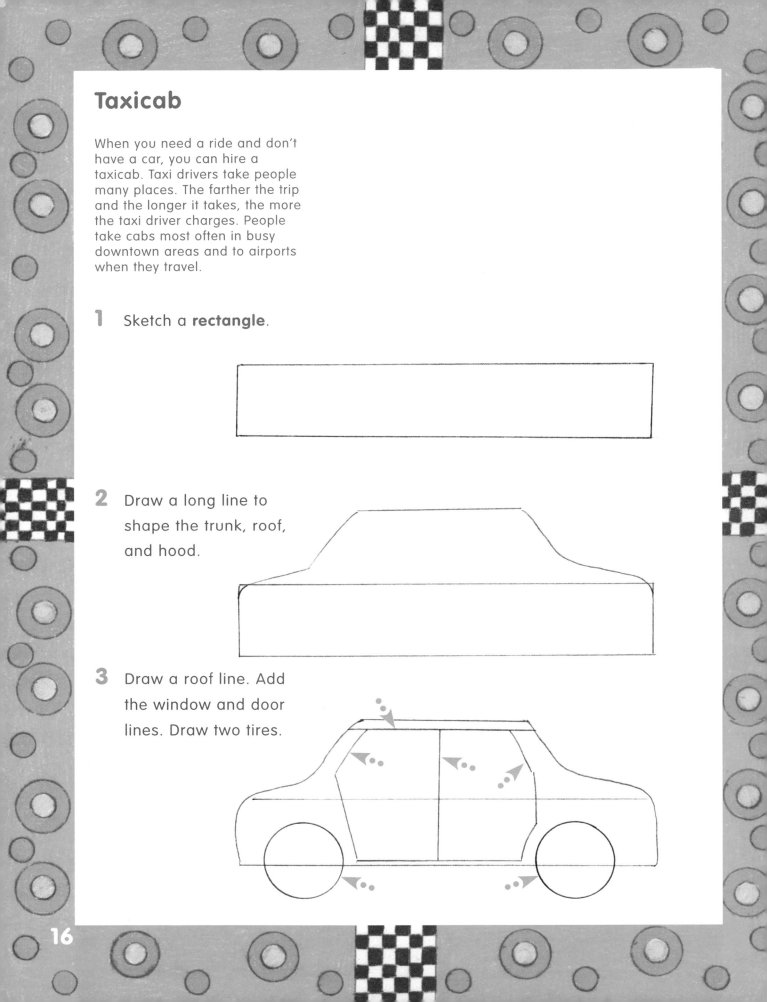

2 Draw a long line to shape the trunk, roof, and hood.

3 Draw a roof line. Add the window and door lines. Draw two tires.

4 Draw the window and windshield lines. In the back, draw the tail light and a bumper. In the front, draw a headlight and a bumper.

5 Put a light on top of your cab. When it's lit, it means the taxi is ready for hire. Add door handles. To decorate the cab, draw a long thin **rectangle** along the side and divide it into squares. Draw the wheels.

6 LOOK at the final drawing! Erase extra lines. Shade and color your taxicab.

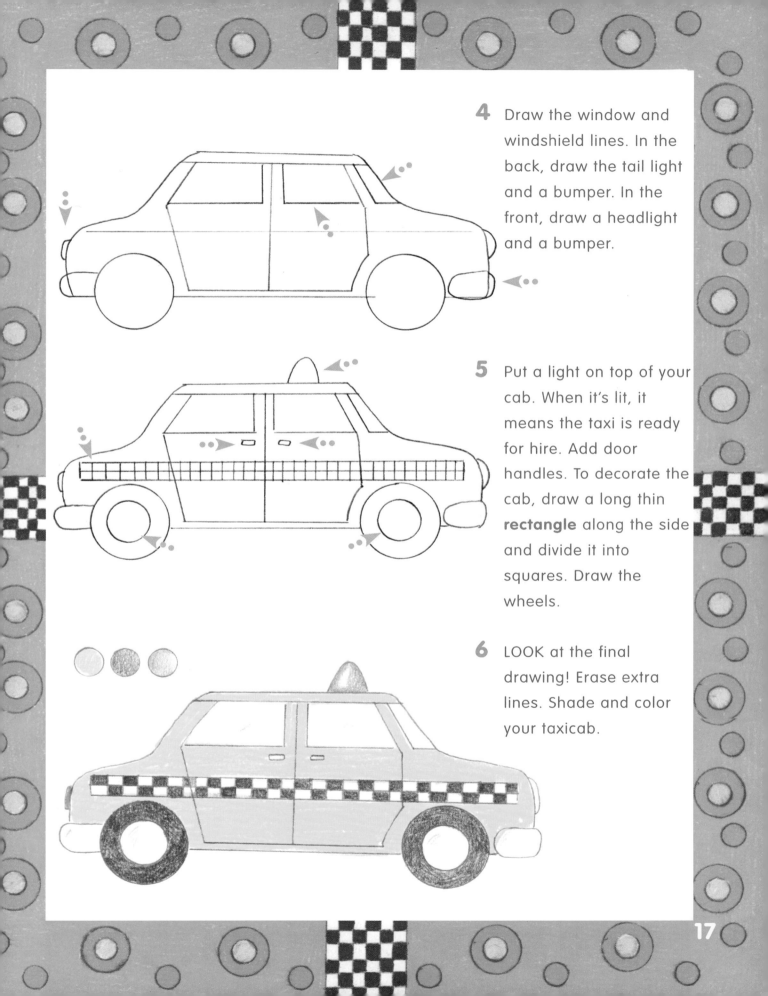

Jeep

The Jeep was originally designed for the army during World War Two. It was a tough little vehicle that could travel on rough roads or go where there were no roads at all. No one is sure where the name Jeep came from. One guess is that it was named after a little character in a Popeye cartoon. The other guess is that it came from the initials "G.P.V." which stood for "General Purpose Vehicle."

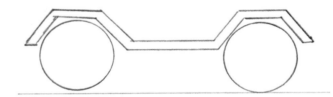

1 To start your Jeep, sketch a ground line. Draw two **circles** touching the line. Look carefully at the shape of the bottom of the chassis. It goes up, across, down, across, up, across, and down. It's a little bit like a long, stretched out "M." Draw it.

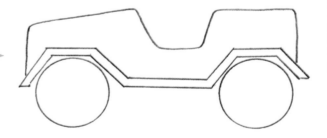

2 Draw the shape of the body. It goes up, across, down, across, up, across and down also.

3 Add a windshield. Draw a steering wheel. Add a seat.

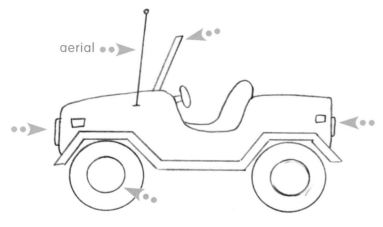

aerial

4 In the front of the Jeep, draw a headlight and a reflector. Add an aerial. In the back of the Jeep, draw a tail light and a reflector. Draw the wheels.

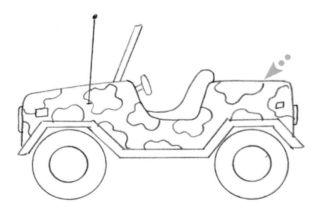

5 Add a camouflage pattern all over the Jeep. Camouflage makes the Jeep harder to see in the woods or in a field.

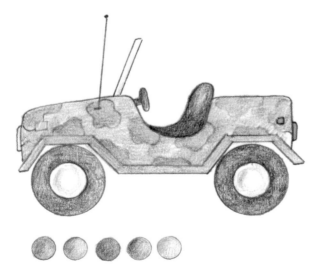

6 LOOK at the final drawing! Erase extra lines. Shade and color your Jeep.

Beetle

1 This little round car starts differently. Instead of a rectangle, it starts with a half **circle**. Sketch a half **circle**.

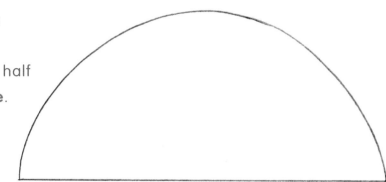

2 Draw the windows which are also half circles. Draw the window supports and a line for the door. Draw two curved fenders that go over the wheels.

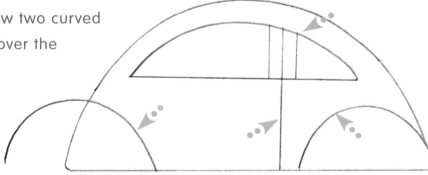

3 Draw a door handle. Add two tires.

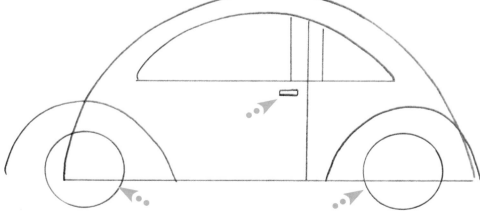

4 Draw a hood. Add a headlight. Draw the wheels. Finish the bottom of the fenders. Add the other door line.

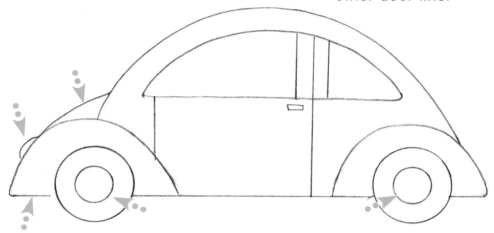

5 LOOK at the final drawing! Erase extra lines. Shade and color your little round car.

My very first car was an orange Volkswagen Beetle. Since then, I have always been fond of little round cars. This one is shaped like the newer version of the Volkswagen Beetle, but all of them look like wind-up toys to me.

Invent Your Own Car

Have fun inventing some car designs of your own. Think of what you want your car to do. Do you want it to go very fast? Be extra tough? Be futuristic? Or just plain silly? Here are a few ideas to get you started.

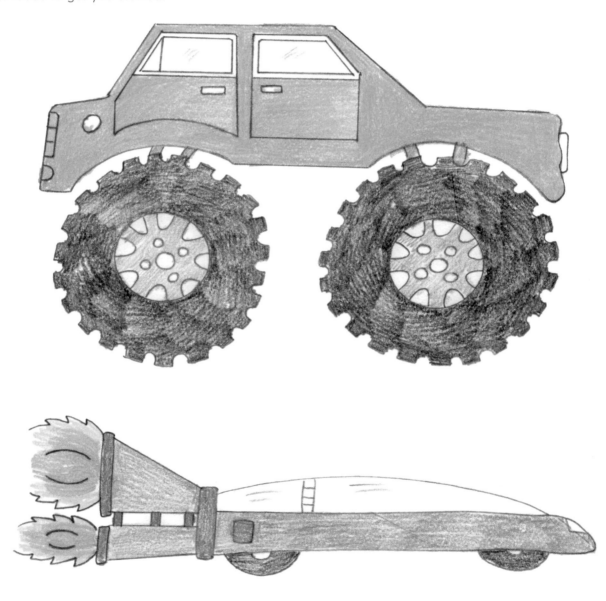

Drawings by Daniel Levin

Drawings by Daniel Levin

Tractor-trailer or "Semi"

A tractor-trailer, sometimes called a "semi," is a really big truck. The biggest are the eighteen-wheelers. They carry all sorts of goods. The driver has a special place inside the truck to sleep on long trips.

1 Sketch a long line on the bottom. On top of the line draw a big rectangle for the trailer, and a small rectangle for the "tractor," or cab.

2 Round off the front of the cab. Draw an exhaust pipe between the cab and body.

3 Add a headlight and bumper to the front of the cab. Draw the chassis underneath the cab of the truck, connecting the front to the back. Draw two tires under the back of the truck, and two tires under the chassis at the front of the truck.

4 Draw the windshield. Draw a door with a window and a door handle.

5 Add stripes across the body of the truck or create your own design. Draw the wheels.

6 LOOK at the final drawing! Erase extra lines. Shade and color your truck.

Terrific truck!

25

Pick-up Truck

A pick-up truck is a smaller truck with a flat, open back. It carries smaller loads such as sacks of feed.

1   Sketch a **rectangle** to start your pick-up truck.

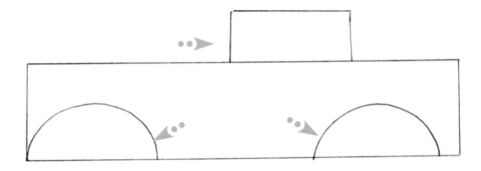

2   Add a **rectangle** on top, toward the front of the truck. Draw two half **circles** for the fenders. Notice where they are placed.

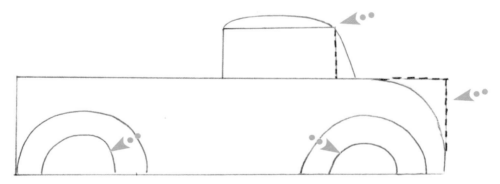

3   Draw a curving line over the top rectangle for the roof of the cab and the windshield. Draw another curved line to shape the hood of the truck. Erase the corner of the long rectangle. Draw a curved line inside the fenders.

4 Draw the windshield. Draw a door with a window and a door handle. Draw two tires and wheels underneath the fenders.

5 Draw a stripe across the body of the truck. Add a bumper, taillight, and reflector to back of the truck. Add a headlight, a reflector, and a bumper to the front of the truck.

6 LOOK at the final drawing! Erase extra lines. Shade and color your pick-up truck. What do you want to haul around? Draw it!

Tow Truck

A tow truck helps when a car breaks down or has been in an accident. A hook is placed under the front bumper of a car and a hoist lifts the car so the tow truck can pull it to a garage.

1 Sketch two **rectangles** to begin the tow truck.

2 Draw a line to cut off the top corner of the back **rectangle**. Draw a smaller **rectangle** at the front of the tow truck and connect the corners of the two front rectangles with a line for the windshield.

3 Add another **rectangle** and a **trapezoid** to the front of the tow truck. Draw a door with a window and a door handle.

trapezoid

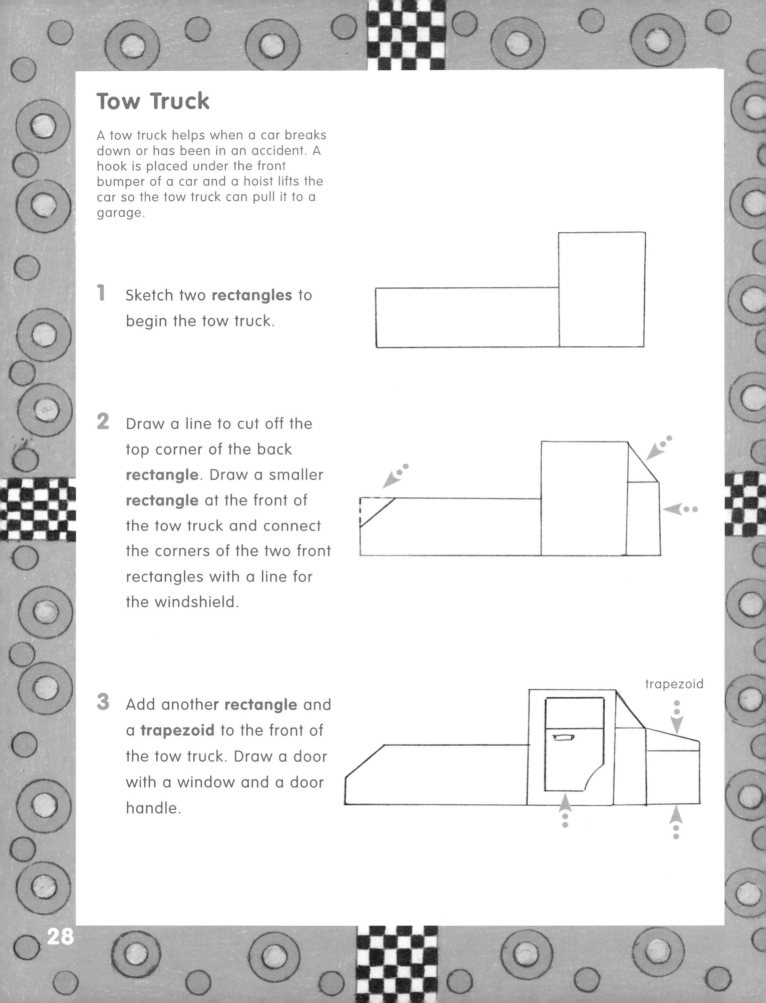

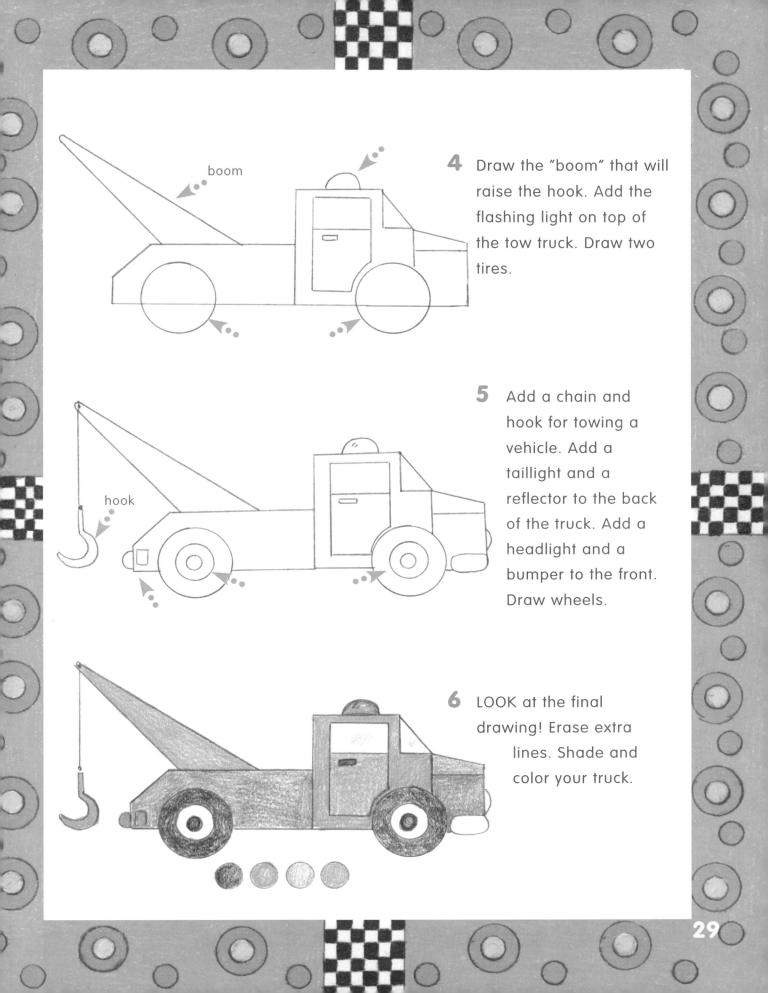

4 Draw the "boom" that will raise the hook. Add the flashing light on top of the tow truck. Draw two tires.

boom

5 Add a chain and hook for towing a vehicle. Add a taillight and a reflector to the back of the truck. Add a headlight and a bumper to the front. Draw wheels.

hook

6 LOOK at the final drawing! Erase extra lines. Shade and color your truck.

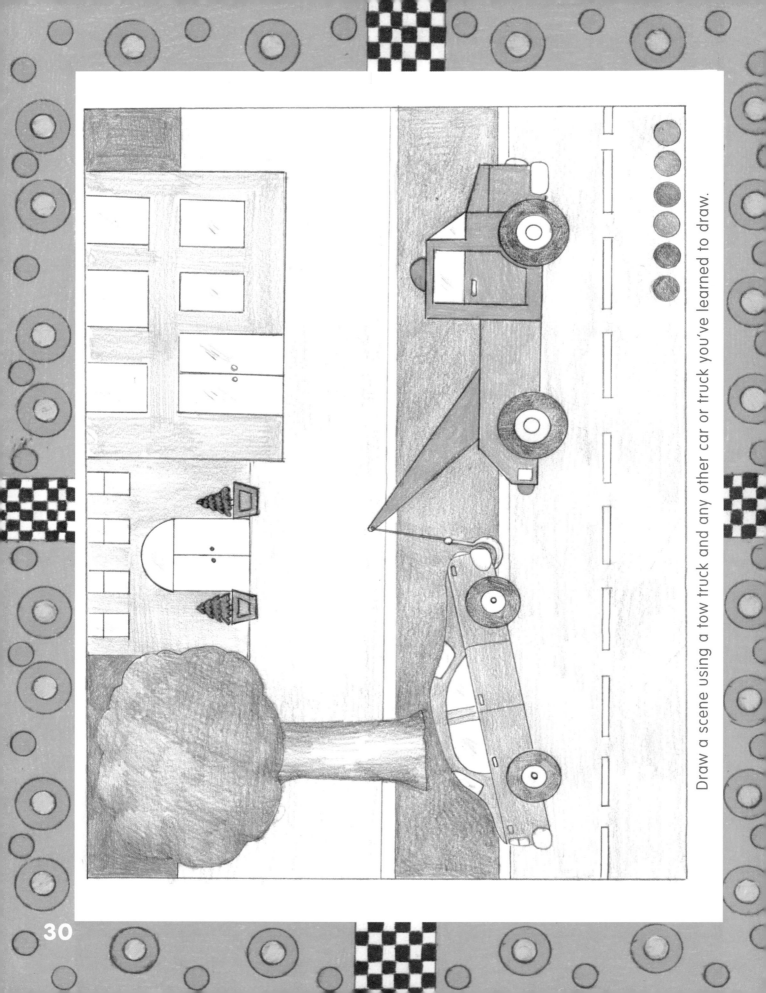

Draw a scene using a tow truck and any other car or truck you've learned to draw.

Camper

A camper is a fun way to take a driving vacation, especially with kids and pets. There are little kitchens to cook a meal, beds to sleep in, and bathrooms with showers and toilets. It's like taking a house along with you.

1 To start your camper, sketch a BIG **rectangle**.

2 Draw a curving line to shape the back of the camper. Draw a curving line at the front for the hood and windshield. Sketch a line for the ground. Draw two tires touching it.

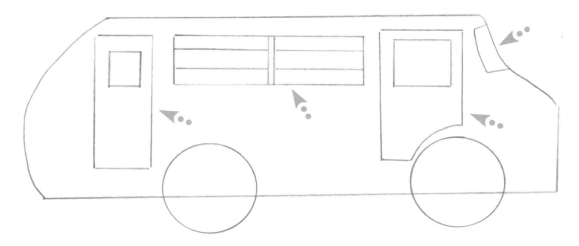

3 Draw doors at the back and front of the camper. Draw windows. Add a windshield.

4 Draw a storage box with straps on the top of the camper. Draw hand rails on the back. Add a bumper to the front.

5   Add reflectors and a taillight to the back. Add a reflector and a headlight to the front. Draw a stripe across the side of the camper. Draw the wheels.

6   LOOK at the final drawing! Erase extra lines. Shade and color your camper.

Happy trails!

Ice Cream Truck

In the summer, my favorite truck is the ice cream truck! It has freezers inside to keep ice cream cold. Sometimes the ice cream truck plays music so everyone knows it's coming.

1 Sketch a big **rectangle** and a little **rectangle**. The little rectangle will be the front of truck.

front

2 Above the smaller rectangle, draw a **triangle** for the windshield. Draw a line to cut off the corner of the rectangle to shape the front of the truck. Draw a door with a window. Draw a **rectangle** window in the middle of the truck with rounded top corners and a ledge underneath.

3 Add a headlight, reflector, and a bumper to the front of the truck. Draw a door handle. Draw a line for an awning over the big window. Below it, add supports for the ledge. Draw a rear bumper, reflectors, and a taillight.

4 Make a sign on top. Draw your favorite treats. Add stripes to the awning. Draw the freezers inside the truck that you can see through the window. Add a sign on the side of the truck. Draw wheels.

5 LOOK at the final drawing! Erase extra lines. Shade and color your ice cream truck.

yum!

Police Car

The police car has flashing lights and a siren to warn you to get out of the way when it is rushing to help people at the scene of a crime or an accident. Cars pull aside when they hear the siren or see the flashing light.

1 To start your police car, sketch a **rectangle**.

2 Draw a long line to shape the trunk, roof, and hood of the car. Draw the **trapezoid** window shape. Add two tires.

trapezoid

3 Draw the back window. Draw the windshield. Draw lines to shape the front and back doors. Add a taillight and rear bumper. Draw the headlight and front bumper.

4 Add a flashing light to the top of the car. Add door handles. Draw the shield on the side of the car. Draw wheels.

5 LOOK at the final drawing! Erase extra lines. Shade and color your police car.

Mail Truck

The mail truck collects and delivers...what else? Mail! The driver collects the mail from the letter boxes and brings it to the post office to be sorted. A special sliding door on the side of the truck allows the driver to pull up to a curb and hop in and out easily.

1 Sketch a boxy **rectangle**.

2 Draw the front shape of the truck and erase the corner of the rectangle. Draw two tires.

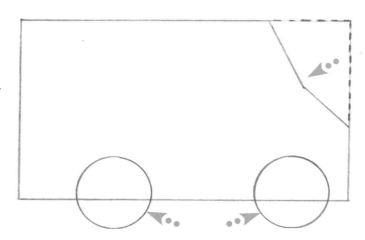

3 Draw a door. Draw a **trapezoid** window. Add two wheels.

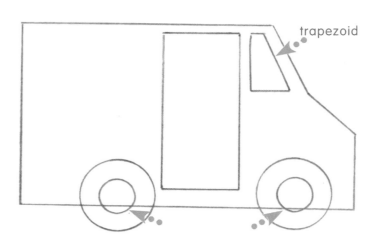

trapezoid

4 Inside the truck, draw a seat for the driver, a line for the floor, and a steering wheel. Add headlights and bumpers to the rear and front of the mail truck.

5 Draw a **rectangle** shape on the side. A poster or picture of a stamp can go here. Add three stripes across the side of the truck. Add reflectors to the front and back.

6 LOOK at the final drawing! Erase extra lines. Shade and color your mail truck.

Garbage Truck

Garbage trucks collect, haul, and dump garbage. Garbage goes into the hopper at the back of the truck. A huge blade pushes the garbage in. To empty the truck, the hopper is tipped up and the garbage is pushed out.

1   Sketch two **rectangles**.

2   Make a line for the windshield. Draw two angled lines at the back of the truck to create the hopper. Erase upper left and right corner sketch lines. Draw part of a tire under the cab. Draw two tires to support the back of the truck.

3   Add two vertical lines to the cab for the window and door. Draw a fender over the front tire. Add wheels to the tires.

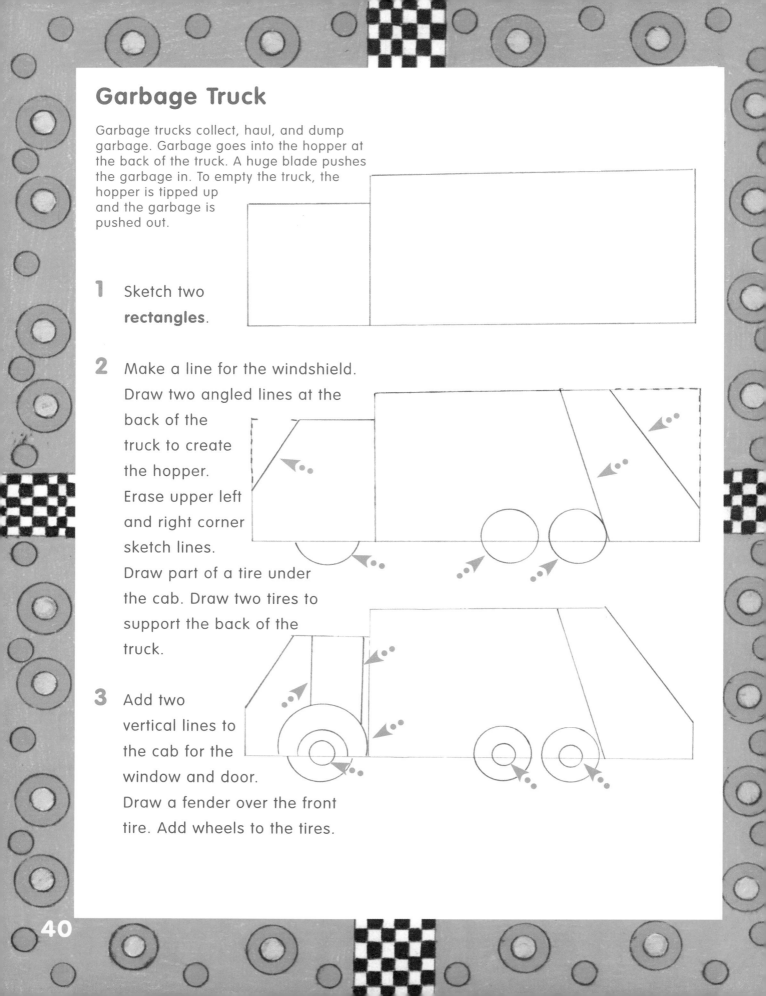

4 Draw a flashing light on the top of the cab. Draw a windshield, a side window, and a door handle. Add a headlight, reflector, and front bumper. On the side of the truck, draw the three shapes you see. Draw the lines on the side of the hopper. Add reflectors and a taillight to the back of the truck.

5 LOOK at the final drawing! Erase extra lines. Shade and color your garbage truck.

Great garbage truck!

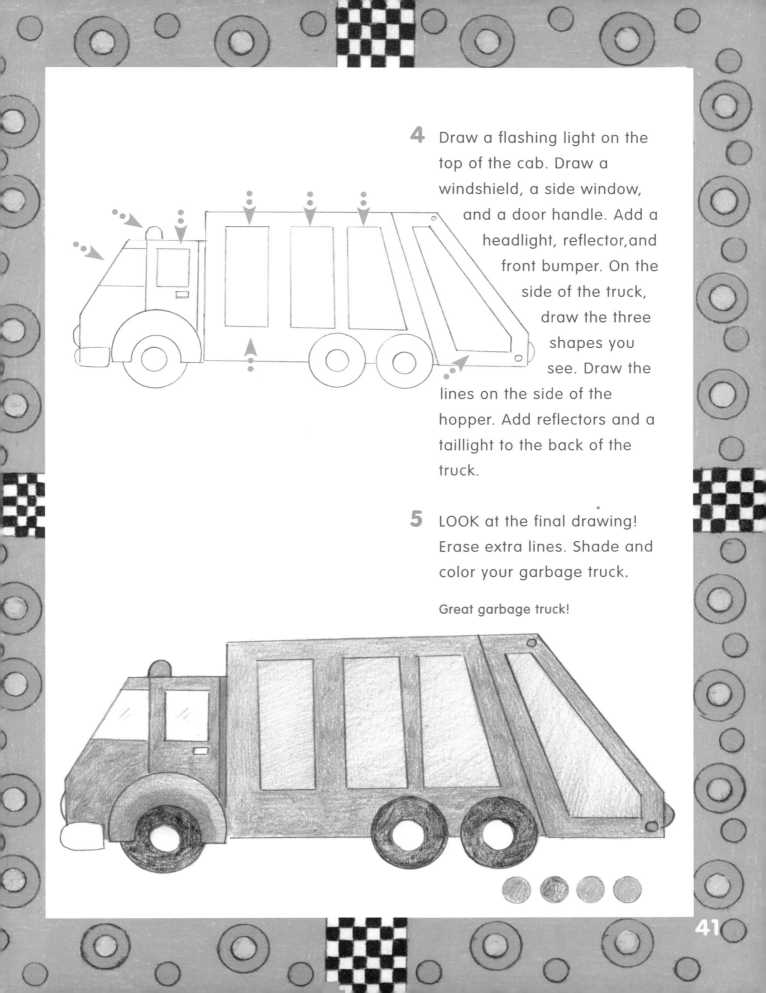

School Bus

This school bus takes many children to school at the same time. Some school buses have lifts so that kids in wheelchairs can ride the bus. When a school bus loads or unloads children, a special stop sign pops out of the side of the bus to let other drivers know they must stop too.

1 Sketch a **rectangle**.

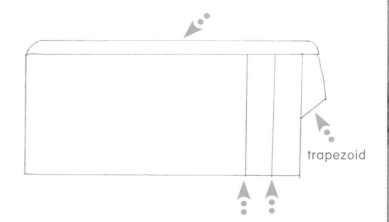

2 Draw a roof on top of the bus. Draw two vertical lines at the front of the bus. These will be doors. Add the **trapezoid** shape of the windshield to the front of the bus.

trapezoid

3 Draw the windows. Add a stripe to the side of the bus. Add windows to the doors.

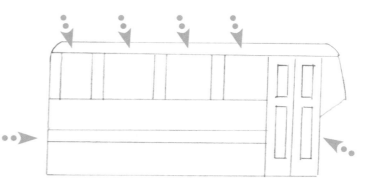

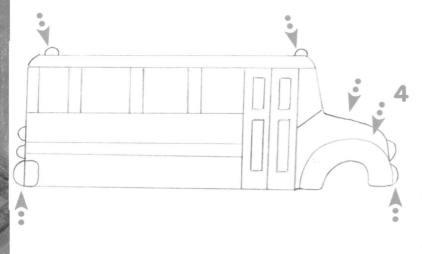

4 Add lights to the roof of the bus. Draw tail lights and a rear bumper. Draw the hood and fender over the front tire to shape the front of the bus. Add a headlight and a front bumper.

5 Draw two tires and wheels.

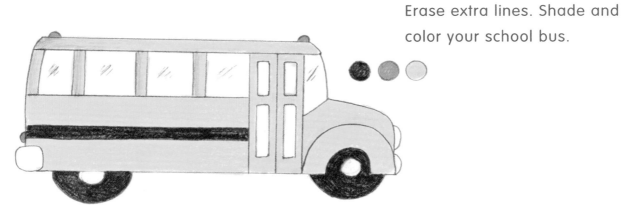

6 LOOK at the final drawing! Erase extra lines. Shade and color your school bus.

Super school bus!

Ambulance

An ambulance rushes to the hospital, carrying people who are sick or injured. In the back of the truck, paramedics give first aid. The ambulance has a loud siren and flashing lights to warn other cars to pull over. The ambulance driver knows every minute counts when someone needs help.

1 Sketch three **rectangles**: one large, one medium, and one small.

2 Draw a line to cut off the corner of the middle rectangle for the windshield. Draw a line to cut off the corner of the smallest rectangle to shape the hood. Draw two tires.

windshield

hood

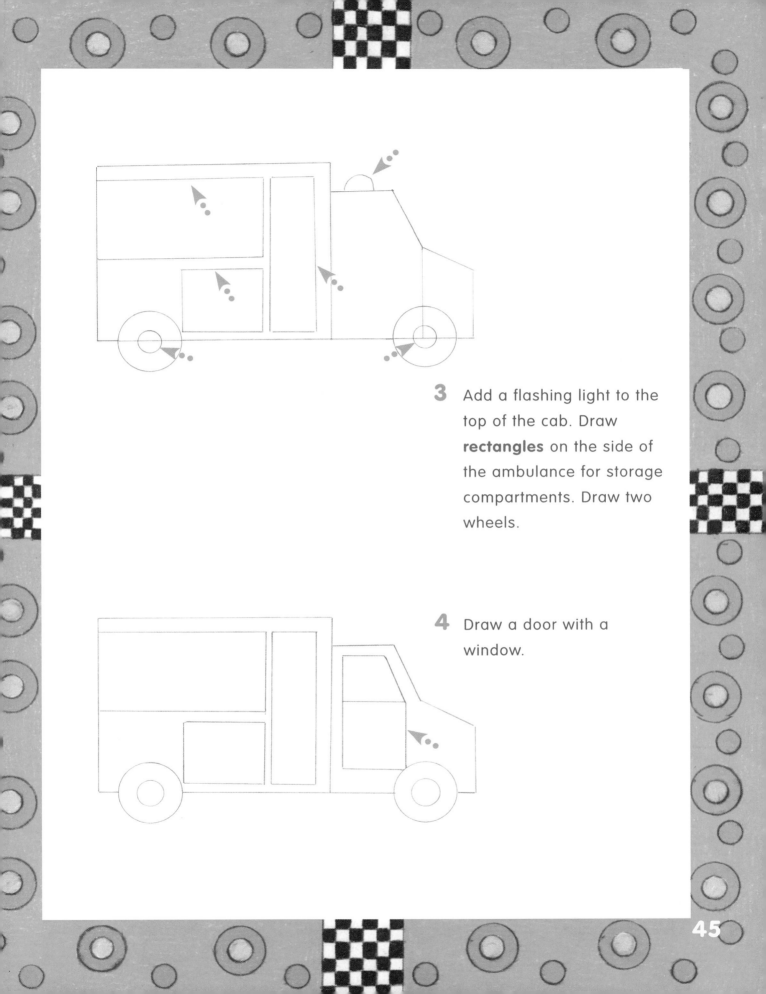

3 Add a flashing light to the top of the cab. Draw **rectangles** on the side of the ambulance for storage compartments. Draw two wheels.

4 Draw a door with a window.

5 Draw reflectors, headlights, tail lights, and bumpers. Draw the door handle. Sketch two **rectangles** to make the red cross on the side of the ambulance. This shows it is a medical vehicle. Draw handles on two of the storage compartments.

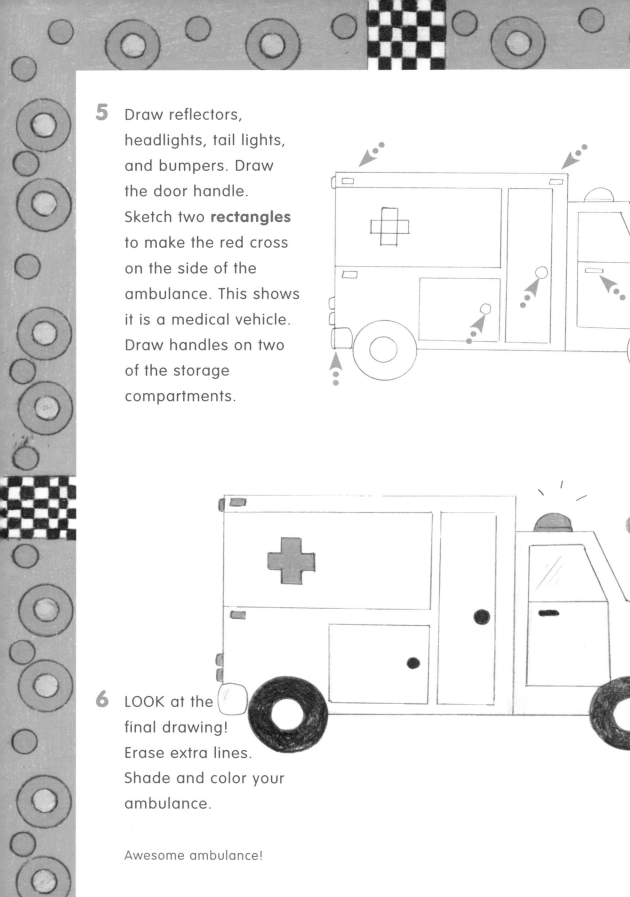

6 LOOK at the final drawing! Erase extra lines. Shade and color your ambulance.

Awesome ambulance!

Fire Truck

Fire trucks also have flashing lights and sirens. Every second counts in putting out fires and saving people's lives.There are several different kinds of fire trucks. Some pump water and some have ladders to reach high to the tops of burning buildings. Some fire trucks carry their own water and some have hoses that attach to fire hydrants.

cab

1   Sketch a line for the ground. Make it light so that you can erase it later. Draw a long, low **rectangle** and a **square** for the cab of the truck.

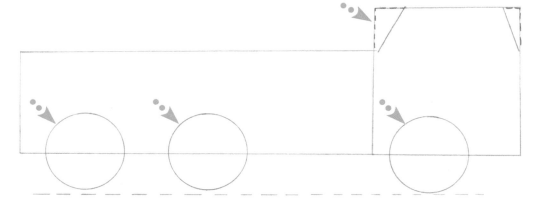

2   Draw lines to shape the top corners of the cab. Add three tires. Notice where the tires are placed. One is under the cab and two are toward the back of the fire truck.

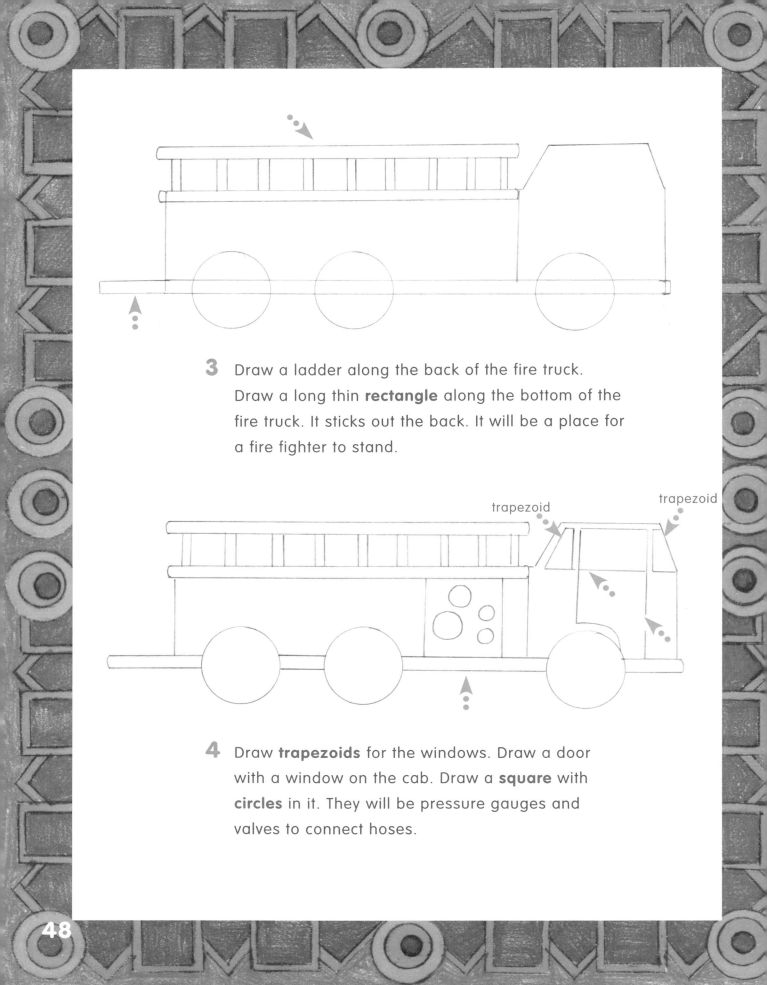

3 Draw a ladder along the back of the fire truck. Draw a long thin **rectangle** along the bottom of the fire truck. It sticks out the back. It will be a place for a fire fighter to stand.

trapezoid

trapezoid

4 Draw **trapezoids** for the windows. Draw a door with a window on the cab. Draw a **square** with **circles** in it. They will be pressure gauges and valves to connect hoses.

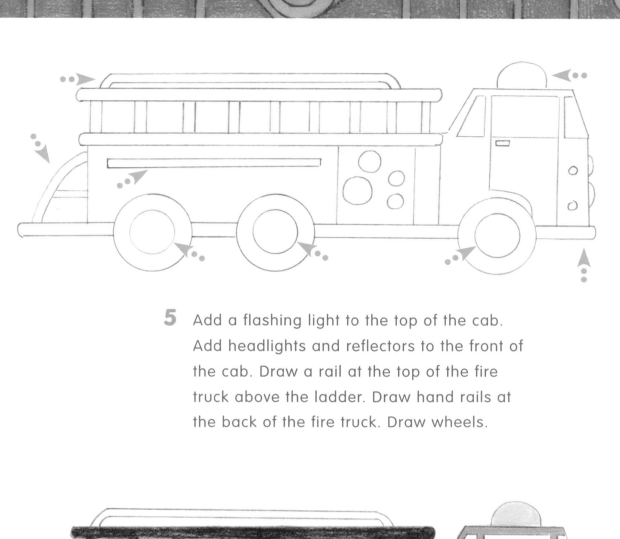

5 Add a flashing light to the top of the cab. Add headlights and reflectors to the front of the cab. Draw a rail at the top of the fire truck above the ladder. Draw hand rails at the back of the fire truck. Draw wheels.

6 LOOK at the final drawing! Erase extra lines. Shade and color your fire truck.

Bookmobile

The bookmobile is a small traveling library. It takes a selection of books to people who cannot get to the library. They borrow the books until the next time the bookmobile is in their neighborhood. A librarian helps them find what they want. Next to the ice cream truck, the bookmobile is my favorite!

1 Sketch a **rectangle**.

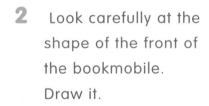

2 Look carefully at the shape of the front of the bookmobile. Draw it.

3 Sketch a light line for the ground. Draw two tires.

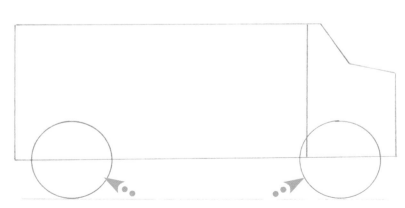

4 Draw a line for the roof. Draw a door at the front for the driver. Add a sliding door to the middle of the bookmobile.

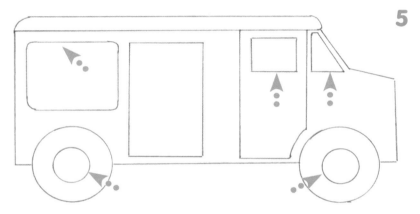

5 Add windows. Draw a **rectangle** sign with rounded corners on the back side. Draw wheels.

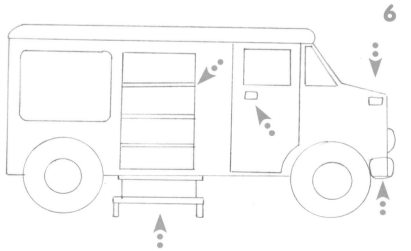

6 Draw a front headlight, reflector and bumper. Add a door handle to the driver's door. Draw shelves inside the bookmobile. Draw steps under the door.

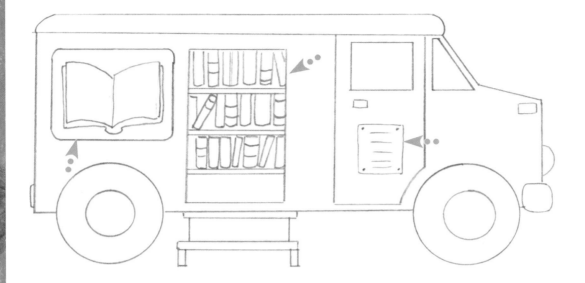

7 Draw a sign on the driver's door telling the schedule. Draw books on the shelves inside the bookmobile. Draw an open book on the sign on the side of the bookmobile.

8 LOOK at the final drawing! Erase extra lines. Shade and color your bookmobile.

Cement Truck

At the building site, workers dig the foundation for a building. When the ground is ready, the cement truck comes. The drum on the back of the truck rolls so the wet cement won't set. Wet cement is emptied into the ground through a chute. It has to be done all at once so the foundation will be strong and won't crack.

1 Sketch an upright **rectangle** for the cab and a long thin **rectangle** for the chassis of the truck.

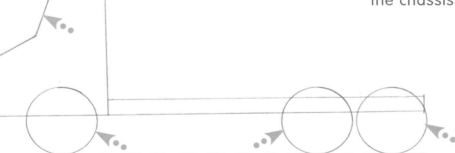

2 Draw lines for the windshield and hood of the cab. Erase the corner of the rectangle. Sketch a line for the ground. Draw three tires. Notice where they are placed.

3 Draw a **rectangle** on an angle.

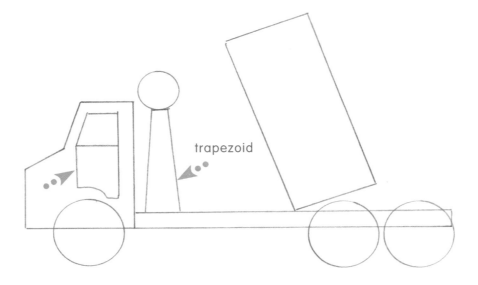

trapezoid

4 Draw a door and window on the cab of the truck. Behind the cab, draw a **trapezoid** topped by a **circle**, the support for the drum.

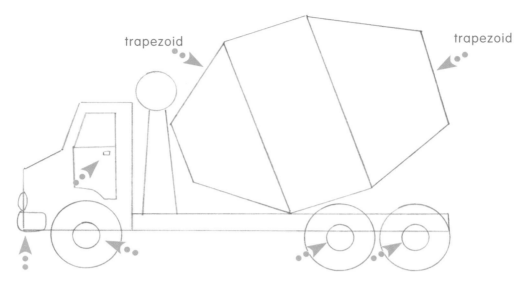

trapezoid

trapezoid

5 Draw a headlight and bumper on the front of the cab. Add a handle to the door. To complete the drum, draw a **trapezoid** on either side of the **rectangle**. Draw the wheels.

6 LOOK at the final drawing! Erase extra lines. Shade and color your cement truck.

Bulldozer

Bulldozers come in many sizes. A fairly little one like this is useful because it can turn around and maneuver in small spaces. It can push and lift stones and rubble. It has crawler treads over its wheels to help it move over bumpy ground.

1 Sketch a big and a small **rectangle** with a little space between them. Draw three wheels.

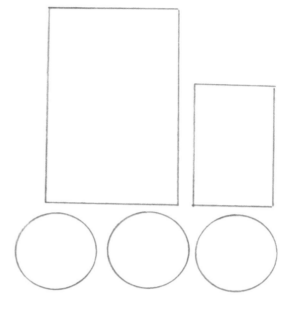

2 Draw a line for the windshield. Erase the corner of the **rectangle**. Add a door with a **trapezoid** window and a handle on the cab of the bulldozer. Draw an exhaust pipe on the top of the smaller **rectangle**. Draw a vent on the side of the smaller **rectangle**. Draw three wheels.

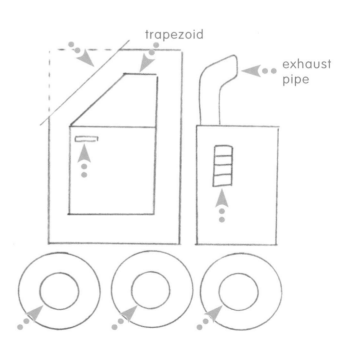

trapezoid

exhaust pipe

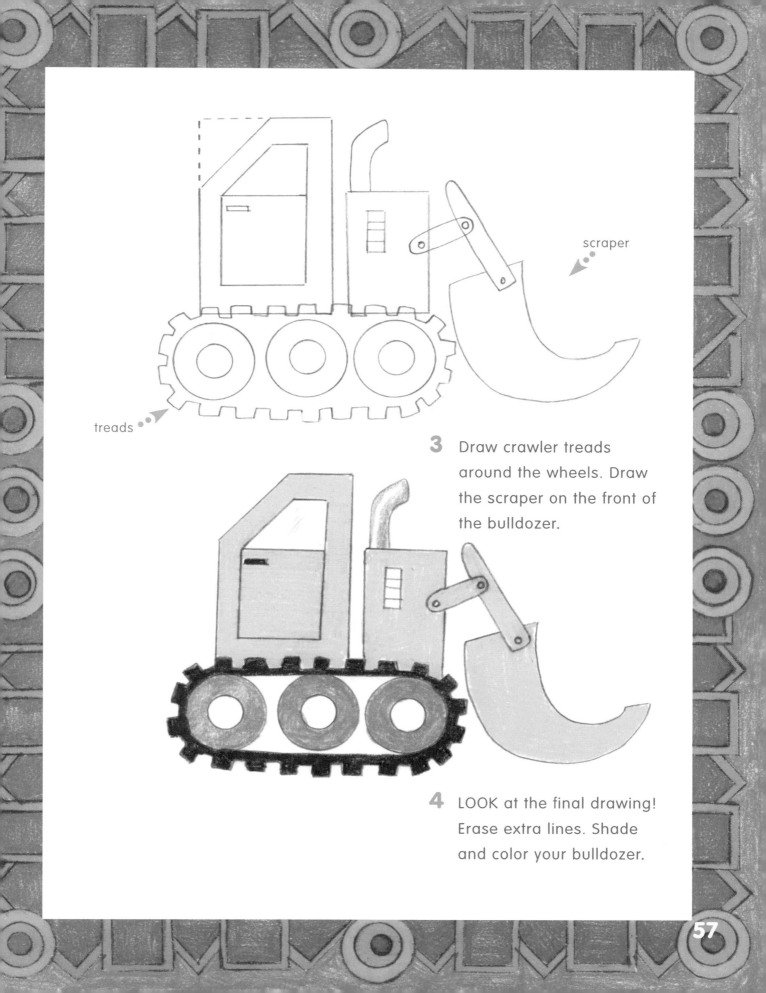

scraper

treads

3 Draw crawler treads around the wheels. Draw the scraper on the front of the bulldozer.

4 LOOK at the final drawing! Erase extra lines. Shade and color your bulldozer.

Back Hoe

A back hoe is a great digger. It has a bucket on the front with teeth to cut into the ground. It makes holes for the foundations of buildings.

1 Sketch a **rectangle**. Draw a line to cut off a corner of the rectangle and erase the point.

trapezoid

2 Draw a **trapezoid** and a small **rectangle** on top of the first **rectangle**.

3 Draw windows and a door on the cab. Under the door, draw a small **rectangle**. Notice its position. Start a **rectangle** under that, but don't finish the bottom yet.

4 Draw three wheels. Draw a line around the wheels to begin the treads.

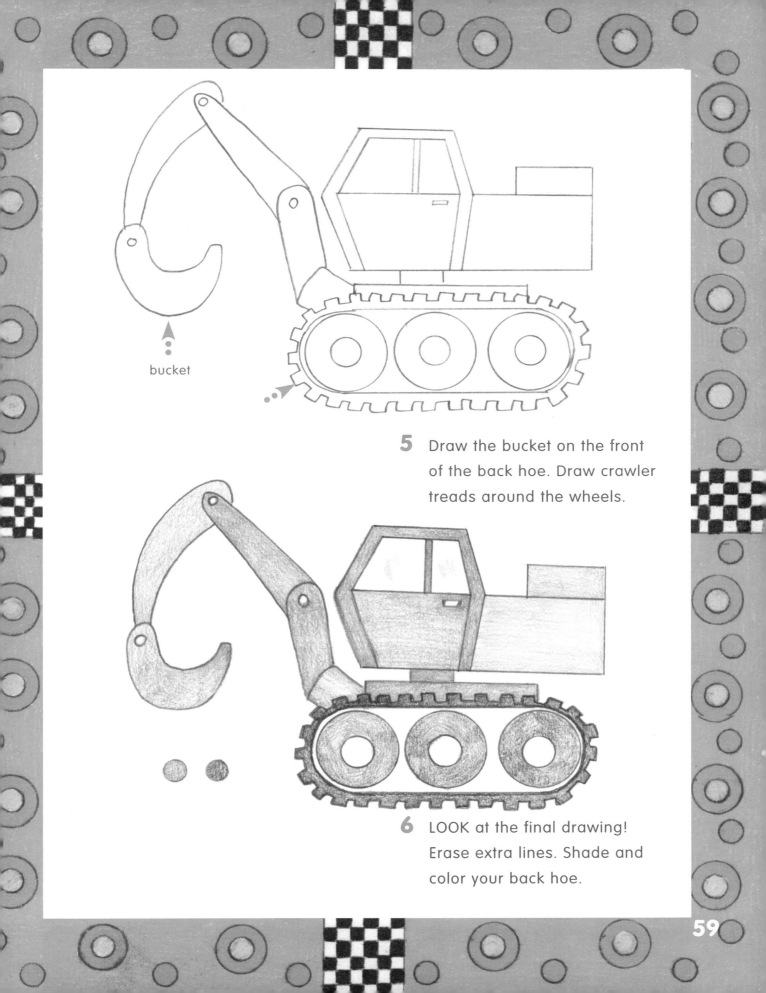

bucket

5 Draw the bucket on the front of the back hoe. Draw crawler treads around the wheels.

6 LOOK at the final drawing! Erase extra lines. Shade and color your back hoe.

Dump Truck

A dump truck is a big truck with a giant box on the back. It hauls stones and dirt away from a construction site and it dumps dirt and gravel where it is needed to fill in holes. The box on the back of the truck is lifted by a hydraulic (hi-draw-lik) shaft. The back of the truck opens to dump its load.

1 Sketch two **rectangles**. The smaller, upright rectangle will be the cab of the truck. The large tipped up rectangle will be the back of the truck. Notice the angle.

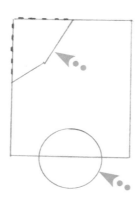

2 Draw lines for the windshield and hood of the cab. Erase the corner of the **rectangle**. Draw three tires. One is under the cab. Two more are under the back of the truck.

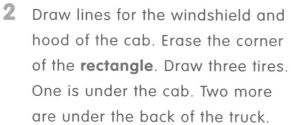

3 Draw a long, thin **rectangle** for the chassis of the truck Add the door and window on the cab.

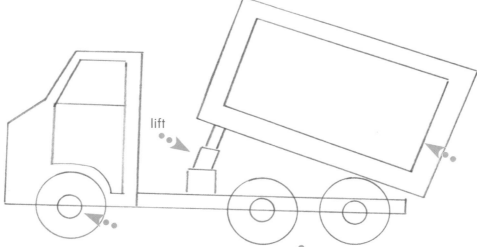

lift

4 Draw the hydraulic lift. Draw an inner **rectangle** inside the box of the truck. Draw the wheels.

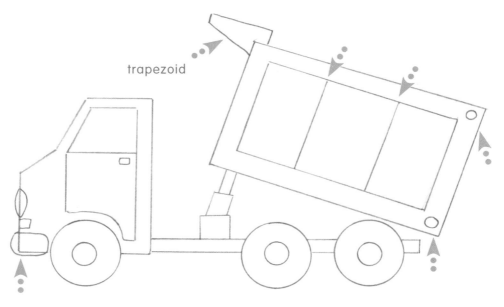

trapezoid

5 Add a headlight, reflector, and bumper to the cab. Draw a **trapezoid** on the upper left hand corner of the box. Divide the inner **rectangle** with two vertical lines. Add reflectors to the back of the truck.

6 LOOK at the final drawing! Erase extra lines. Shade and color your dump truck.

Have fun drawing machines at your own construction site!

Index

Learn about other drawing books online at www.drawbooks.com!